CROSS YOUR FINGERS, SPIT IN YOUR HAT

For Calliope
and Andrew

Besides, there are a hundred things one has to know, which we all understand about and you don't, as yet. I mean pass-words, and signs, and sayings which have power and effect, and plants you carry in your pockets, and verses you repeat . . . all simple enough when you know them, but they've got to be known . . . or you'll find yourself in trouble.

Kenneth Grahame,
The Wind in the Willows

CROSS YOUR FINGERS, SPIT IN YOUR HAT

Superstitions and Other Beliefs
Collected by ALVIN SCHWARTZ
Illustrated by GLEN ROUNDS

HarperCollins*Publishers*

"Besides, there are a hundred things…" (p. 3) is reprinted from *The Wind in the Willows*, Kenneth Grahame, by permission of Charles Scribner's Sons. Copyright 1908 by Charles Scribner's Sons.

The account of the wart witch (p. 97) is reprinted from "The Magic Art of Removing Warts," Grace P. Wellborn, a chapter in *Singers and Storytellers*, by permission of the Texas Folklore Society. Copyright © 1961 by Texas Folklore Society.

The account of Dr. Gordon and the ghost dog (pp. 126-127) is reprinted from *Ozark Superstitions*, Vance Randolph, by permission of the Columbia University Press. Copyright 1947 by Columbia University Press.

Every reasonable effort has been made to obtain appropriate permission to reprint materials already in copyright. If the editor or publisher is notified of omissions, corrections will be made in future editions.

U.S. Library of Congress Cataloging in Publication Data

Schwartz, Alvin, birth date   comp.
Cross your fingers, spit in your hat.

SUMMARY: Superstitions about such topics as love and marriage, money, ailments, travel, the weather, and death.
Bibliography: p.
1. Folklore—Juvenile literature. 2. Superstition—Juvenile literature.
[1. Superstition] I. Rounds, Glen, birth date   illus. II. Title.
GR74.S37   1974   001.9′6   73-21912
ISBN-0-397-31530-9   ISBN-0-397-31531-7 (pbk.)
ISBN-0-397-32436-7 (lib. bdg.)

Contents

Good Lucks and Bad Lucks

When the boys and girls in Severna Park, Maryland, talk about their superstitions they call them "good lucks and bad lucks," which is a good description, for that is what superstitions are all about.

As always has been the case, there are a great many people who are superstitious. To make sure of their luck they carry a lucky coin, or cross their fingers, or take other steps they think are needed. But most will not admit to it, for in this day and age it makes them feel silly.

Yet there are in this country more than a million superstitions on which people depend. Together they make up the largest part of our folklore.

Many are so old we do not know what they are based on or where they come from. But they tell us how to find good luck, or how to protect ourselves from evil, or how to learn what lies ahead.

They also involve a kind of magic through which we give a coin or a plant or a star, or whatever, the power to meet our needs.

We rely on superstitions for the same reasons people always have. When we are faced with situations we cannot control—which depend on "luck" or "chance"—superstitions make us feel more secure. Many also are funny and give us pleasure. And many are the stuff of which hopes and dreams are made.

Alvin Schwartz

Princeton, New Jersey

CROSS YOUR FINGERS, SPIT IN YOUR HAT

Love and Marriage

Pull a hair from the head of someone
you love, and he will love you deeply.

He also will love you if he eats a bowl of soup to which you secretly have added three drops of your blood, or if he drinks a glass of lemonade to which you have added your fingernail filings or in which you have soaked your toenail clippings.

The number of times you can pop your knuckle equals
the number of boys who now love you.

Whether you will marry is, of course, another
question.

If you are strong enough to break an apple in
half with your bare hands,
    or you kiss somebody with a moustache
and get a hair in your mouth,
    or you eat the point of a piece of pie
before you eat the rest,
    or you step on a cat's tail,
    you probably will not.

But if you stumble going up a flight of stairs,
    or you have hairy legs,
    or the lines in your palm form the letter M,
    or you dream of taking a bath,
    you probably will.
    In fact, if you sit on a table, you will marry
before you are able.

You will dream of what your future husband looks
like if you sleep with a mirror under your pillow.
This also will happen if you count nine stars
each night for nine nights,
or you wear your nightgown inside out,
or you rub your bed posts with lemon peels before
you turn your lights off.

If you soak a shoelace in water, then throw it at the
ceiling, the mark it leaves will look like his initial.

If you fill your mouth with water and run around the block three times, you will learn his name. For the first person you see after you stop will have the name of your future husband.

And you will learn even more if you try this.

Write your name on a piece of paper. Under it write the name of the person you want most to marry. Then cross out any letters in your name that also are in his name. For example:

$ΨSΑN FRØBΙSHΕR JONΕ$
$ΑMΨΕL HΑRRΙNGTØN $MITH

When you cross out the first pair of letters, say "love"; the second, "friendship"; the third, "hatred"; the fourth, "marriage." Then start over. When you are finished, you will know where you stand with *that* person.

But none of this is necessary if you manage to eat one hundred chicken gizzards at a time, or if you swallow whole the raw heart of a chicken. For if you can do that, you can marry anyone you want to.

If you do marry, there will be a wedding. And if it is like most, it will involve many customs so old we have forgotten what they mean or how they came to be. For example:

The bride's veil. At one time the bride wore a veil to protect herself. In some cases she feared that a person who was jealous of her happiness might harm her with the evil eye. But she also used a veil to disguise herself so that evil spirits would not know who she was. For they hated weddings and did everything they could to make trouble.

A maid of honor, a best man, bridesmaids, ushers. One reason they participate is an old Roman custom that every wedding have at least ten witnesses. Another reason also involves evil spirits. To make it harder for them to figure out just who was being married, the bride and the groom surrounded themselves with friends who were dressed the way they were.

A wedding cake. This is one custom whose meaning has not changed. The cake still represents a wish that a newly married couple will have the good things of life.

Rice. Since rice grows in great abundance, guests at weddings long ago threw great handfuls at the bride and groom to make certain they would have many children and much food.

Horns and bells. Years ago these were not used to celebrate, but to drive away with their noise any evil spirits who still had not given up.

Old shoes. Now we tie them to the back of a car so that everyone will know that the people inside have just gotten married. But at one time the bride's father gave her old shoes to her new husband as a sign that *he* was now responsible for her. In some cases the groom then hit his bride on the head with a shoe to make sure she understood. But today, of course, he wouldn't dare.

Children

How many will you have?

The number of lines in your forehead may tell you. So may the number of X's in your palm.

So may the number of seeds in the seed head of a dandelion after you have blown on it three times.

So may an apple. Spit all the seeds you find in one into your palm, then slap them against your forehead. The number that stick is the number of children you may have.

If you trip on a flight of stairs, however, you will have triplets.

If you have a bald-headed baby with big feet, it will get straight A's.

If it has a big mouth, it will be a good singer.

If it has big ears, it will be generous.

If it has curly hair, it will be lucky.

If it is born on a Sunday or on New Year's Day or during a full moon, or if it has a full set of teeth when it arrives, it also will be lucky.

But if it has only one tooth, it will be a vampire.

To help a baby rise in the world, carry him up a flight of stairs before you carry him down.

Also, do not cut his fingernails for a year. Bite them. It will keep him from becoming a thief.

Also, hang a bag of chopped onions around his neck. It will ward off evil.

Also, do not let him sit on rocks. Otherwise, he will become hard-hearted.

To find what else the future holds for your child, place these things on the floor in front of him: a spoon, a dollar, a deck of cards, a book, a Bible, a baseball, a coin, a diaper.

Then watch closely to see which he reaches for first.

If it is the spoon, he will be poor; the dollar, rich; the cards, a gambler; the book, a teacher; the Bible, a preacher; the baseball, an athlete; the coin, a businessman.

If it is the diaper, he will have children of his own.

The Household

If you come in one door and go out another,
or you sleep with your closet door open,
or you hang anything on a doorknob,
or you hop downstairs on one foot,
you are in for trouble.
But if you run around your house three times, it will
improve your luck.

You also will have good luck if you sleep with an ax under your bed and a knife under your pillow. But if you don't get out of bed on the right side, you will have problems. For the left side always has attracted evil.

It also is bad luck to sleep on a table.

And it is risky to spin a chair on one leg. Unless you remember to spin it in the opposite direction, you will have a fight.

But the biggest problem with furniture is mirrors. If you look in one and a friend looks over your shoulder, your friendship will end. And if you drop one and it breaks, your troubles have just begun.

If you break a mirror, it means seven years of bad luck, and for good reason.

When early man saw his reflection in a pond or a lake, he thought what he saw was part of him. And when the wind rippled the water and shattered his image, he was sure he also would have trouble. This is how men later felt when they broke a mirror that once held their image.

But if this happens to you, there are ways to protect yourself.

One is to wait seven hours before you remove the pieces. Another is to throw them into a deep, swiftly moving river where people do not swim. Another is to bury them in a graveyard at midnight when there is no moon and there are no stars.

If someone drops something on you while you are walking under a ladder, that is truly bad luck. However, many people will not walk under a ladder at any time, even though they cannot explain why.

But long ago people had their reasons. One involved death. Before the gallows was invented, murderers were hung from the topmost rungs of ladders. And when they died, it was said their ghosts remained for long periods where they had fallen, which helped make ladders unpopular places.

Another reason involved life. In many religions the symbol of life was a triangle. When a ladder rested against a wall, it formed this symbol. But if someone walked under a ladder, he broke the triangle, disrupted life, and invited the worst kind of trouble.

If you "break" a triangle, walk backward under the ladder to where you started. This will erase what happened and give you another chance.

You will have good luck, however, if you find a pin and take the proper steps. As this old rhyme explains:

See a pin and pick it up,
And all day long you'll have good luck.
See a pin and let it lie,
To good luck you'll say good-bye.

All of which actually has to do with witches, since they use bits and pieces of metal to cast their spells. If you come upon a pin, therefore, and let it lie, a witch might find it, which could be bad luck for somebody.

But if the pin points away from you, don't touch it. Circle it until it points toward you. Then pick it up—and keep it.

If you must leave your old house and move to a new one, do not take your broom with you.

And do not take your cat unless you wave it at some friends when you leave, and pass it through a window when you arrive, and butter its paws so that it stays put.

And do not take your pig trough.

And do not move on Friday.

Food and Drink

If someone in your family can make his first and fourth fingers touch over the back of his hand, he is a good cook.

Encourage him to cook a chicken, for every chicken has a bone which can help you get your wish. Officially it is called the collarbone. But it is better known as the wishbone or the pulleybone.

If you find one while you are eating, you will need somebody to help you use it. First, both of you must make a secret wish. Then each must grab an opposite end of the bone and pull and twist until it breaks.

The one who gets the bigger piece will get his wish. The other must tell what his wish was.

Almost twenty-five hundred years ago people who lived in what today is northern Italy also used a chicken to make a wish come true.

First they dried its collarbone in the sun. Then a person with a wish or a problem touched it and asked the gods for help.

If you eat peas
on New Year's Day,
or black-eyed peas
and hog jowl,
or corn bread
and hog's head,

you will have good luck
all year long.
If they are cooked with a dime,
you will have even better luck.

But if at any time you dream of eating
cabbage, no good will come of it.

Be careful not to waste salt.

Do not spill any.

Do not drop any.

Do not give any away.

In addition, do not hand anyone a shaker of salt. Place it in front of him so that *he* will run the risk of spilling it.

If you forget these rules, throw a pinch of salt over your left shoulder. Otherwise, you will have bad luck, which years ago you would have deserved.

For at one time man depended on salt to keep his food from spoiling and to keep himself alive. When he wasted salt, he saw it as a sign that evil spirits were about.

To protect himself he threw a pinch over his left shoulder, for it was on the left that these spirits lurked. Since salt defended him against death, he reasoned, it would defend him against evil.

Each
time
you
eat
a banana
you
will
grow
taller.

Each time you also can make a wish. To
learn if it will come true, cut a thin slice
from the bottom of the banana where it
grew from the stalk. If you find a spot in
the shape of a Y, it will.

Whoever eats the last piece of food
during a meal must kiss the cook.

Clothing

If you are a girl and a butterfly lands on you, you will get a new dress.

This also will happen if you catch the first butterfly you see in the spring and bite off its head.

Or if the hem of a dress you are wearing turns up and you spit on it.

It is good luck to throw a shoe over your left shoulder without looking.

But it is bad luck to break a shoelace, particularly the left one. And it is even worse to walk with one shoe off and one shoe on. Some say you will have a year of trouble for each step you take.

When you get dressed in the morning,
be sure to put on
your right sock and right shoe
before you put on
your left sock and left shoe,
and you will have a good day.
If, by mistake,
you put on a sweater
or some other clothing
backward or inside out,
it also is good luck.
But you must wear it that way all day
or your good luck will turn bad.
The only exception to this rule
is your underwear.
You can turn it right side out
just after lunch.

If all you've had is bad luck and what you want is
good luck, first turn your hat around, then pull your
pockets out, and things will get better sooner than you
think.

Friends and Neighbors

If you drop
a knife,
a fork,
or a spoon,
or your cat
washes its face,
or you sneeze
before breakfast,
or you pour
a glass of water
and it is
full of bubbles,
company's coming.

If you drop a dirty, greasy dishrag, somebody who probably is dirtier and greasier than you are is on his way. If you drop it twice, he will stay for dinner.

But if he stays too long, put a pinch of pepper under his chair or stand a broom behind a door, and he will leave.

If you and a friend
say the same thing at the same time,
do not speak another word
until you hook your thumbs
or little fingers,
make a wish,
and repeat this rhyme:

Needles, pins,
Triplets, twins,
When a man marries,
His troubles begins.

When a man dies,
His troubles ends.
What goes up the chimney?
Smoke.
Your wish and my wish
May never be broke.

And your wish will be granted,
and so will your friend's.

But if the two of you wash your feet or hands
in the same basin at the same time,
   or dry yourselves with the same towel at the
same time,
   you may never speak to each other again.

If you go for a walk with a friend
and a tree or a pole or anything else
comes between you,
you also will quarrel
unless you both say at the same time,
"Salt and pepper!" or
"Bread and butter!"
or you walk back to where you separated
and start over.

When it is time to go home, it is good luck to get a
last look at your friend *after* he has gotten a last look at
you. Call out, "Last look, you dirty crook!" Then disappear.

Witches

If you have a friend or a neighbor who has four joints in her fingers instead of three,

and cannot step over a broom that has been placed in her path,

and cannot stand up when you put a pair of open scissors under her chair,

she could be a witch.

And you'd better watch out.

If she *is* one and you make her angry, she could
cause you to crawl up a wall and leave you there.

Or she could make it impossible for you to sit down
or stand up.

Or she could put a spell on your sewing machine so
that it won't sew,

or on your cow so that she won't give milk,

or on your garden or your field so that nothing
will grow there.

Or she could make you sick,

or drive you crazy,

or kill you,

among other things.

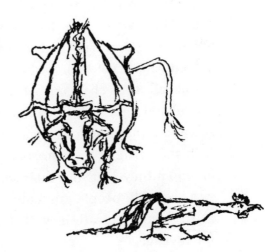

There was a time when nobody thought witches were evil. They were regarded as rather pleasant women whose magic rituals and contacts with various gods helped people get their wishes and solve their problems.

But all this changed when the Christian religion spread and with it the idea that there was only one God. It was not make-believe pagan gods who helped witches with their magic, the Christians said. It was the Devil, to whom they had sold their souls.

As a result, people gradually came to think of witches as frightening creatures with terrible powers they used for revenge.

It was said they flew about on broomsticks, turned into animals to perform their mischief, and had the help of black cats which actually were demons or the Devil himself.

Some witches also were known to make themselves invisible by putting a special cat's bone in their mouths. And at least a few were said to own magic mirrors in which they could see their enemies, no matter where these people might be.

What frightened people most, however, was that a witch might be living next door, and they might not know it until it was too late.

If you would like to become a witch and your mother already is one, you will inherit her powers. But if she is not a witch, there *are* other ways. Three methods are described below. However, each will work only if it is used in secret and at midnight and in total darkness, and if you are sincere.

Repeat the Lord's Prayer backward and shoot seven silver bullets at the moon. These can be made by melting silver coins.

Put one hand on the heel of your left foot and the other on the top of your head and shout everything you can think of that is awful and evil. Then swear that you will forever work in behalf of the Devil. Say, "I give thee all between my hands."

Obtain a totally black cat which has died of old age. Cut off its head with one clean blow of a sword. Then place a pea seed in each of its eyes and bury the head where no one will find it. When the seeds produce peas, cook them and eat them.

If everything goes as it should, the Devil will contact you. And with his teeth he will make a mark, the Devil's mark. But bear in mind that once you decide to join him, there is no turning back.

To be sure that a witch does not harm you, draw a circle around yourself. Or spit in your hat or your right shoe. Or carry the right eye of a wolf in your right hand.

To be sure that a witch does not enter your home, drive three nails into your front door so that they form a triangle.

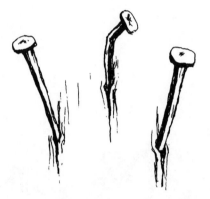

Or you can fasten a horseshoe over the door. For the right procedure, see page 104.

If none of this helps and through bad luck you are bewitched, there are ways to break the spell. Here is one that has worked in many cases.

Add one package of pins and one package of needles to a large pot of boiling water. Then wait patiently. The pins, the needles, and the boiling water will cause the witch such pain that eventually she will appear at your door and plead for mercy. But give her none until she removes the spell and promises never again to harm you.

School

If you sleep with a school book under your pillow, it will help you to learn your lesson. Just be sure the book is opened to the right chapter.

But if you drop the book on the way to school, you will forget everything you learned unless you kiss it before you pick it up.

When you have to take a test, take these steps to
help you pass:

Don't shave.

Wear your socks and underwear inside out
and your shirt or blouse backward.

Carry with you a lucky rock or dog tooth
or some other charm you depend on.

Step on every crack in the sidewalk
on your way to school, or don't step on any.

Use the same pen or pencil you used
the last time you passed a test,
or use a new one that has never made a mistake.

Sit at the same desk you sat at last time.

Cross your legs.

If you still think you will have trouble, swallow a live goldfish. It will make you even more intelligent.

Work

If an actor whistles while he is backstage, he will fall on his face while he is on stage, or he will forget his lines or make some other error.

He also will have bad luck if somebody wishes him good luck,

or if fresh flowers or a rocking chair or the feather of a peacock is part of the scenery,

or if part of his costume is yellow,

or if his shoes squeak.

If a basketball player sinks his last shot during the warm-ups before a game, he will score against the other team.

If a baseball player wears a piece of chewing gum on the top of his cap, he will get a hit.

But if he taps his bat on home plate or changes bats after two strikes have been called, or if somewhere on the field two bats are crossed, he will strike out.

If a prize fighter carries a pickle during a fight, he will get knocked out.

If a racing driver eats peanuts or talks to a woman before a race, he also can expect trouble.

If you decide to go fishing and meet a pig on the way, you will not catch any fish.

But if you play the fiddle, and you fiddle as you fish, you will catch more than you would believe.

If you build a building, be sure to put a coin or some other lucky object inside the walls. Usually it is placed in a corner-stone where two walls meet.

It is today an old custom, but once it was a matter of life or death. At that time an earth god owned the soil, and anyone who used it for any purpose had to pay him or face disaster.

When a new building went up, offerings of food or treasure often were sealed inside the walls. But in ancient Rome the earth god demanded blood, and living children were used.

If a sailor begins a voyage on a Friday,

or if he sails aboard a ship whose name has been changed or whose cargo includes a corpse,

he can expect trouble.

This also is true if he drops a map or a bucket overboard.

He also must be careful not to whistle, for he could whistle up a storm.

But if there is a child aboard, it will be a good voyage.

Money

If your eyebrows grow together or your arms are hairy, you will be very rich.

If there is a mole on your neck,
It means money by the peck.

If your palm itches, it means that money is on its way. To make sure it arrives, put your hand in your pocket or scratch it on a piece of wood.

Money also will be yours if you see a shooting star
and call, "Money, money, money!" before it is gone,

or you bury a coin in a deep hole and leave it there,

or you wear a dime in each of your shoes on New
Year's Day,

or you find bubbles on top of a glass of milk and
swallow them before they break,

or a honeybee zips around your head,

or a tiny red spider lands on you and you don't
harm it,

or you are patient enough to count one hundred
white horses,

or you dream of clear water

or of lots of fish.

If none of this works, spit
over your little finger.

Numbers

13

If you are like lots of people, you have a case of triskaidekaphobia. That is, the number 13 makes you uneasy.

To start a journey on the thirteenth of any month,

to buy or use or give thirteen of anything,

to wear 13 on a uniform,

to eat with twelve others,

to live on a street or in a house or an apartment numbered 13,

to work on the thirteenth floor of a building—

all these are said to mean bad luck.

In many places, in fact, a street or a house or an apartment which should be numbered 13 is given a different number to avoid the risk.

Few people today are able to explain why 13 has such a bad reputation.

One reason may involve the death of Jesus Christ. After He and twelve of His followers—or thirteen in all —ate together, then one of the thirteen betrayed Him to His enemies, and He was killed.

Some scholars say that witches also may be responsible, since they gathered regularly with their black cats in groups of thirteen to plot their evil acts.

3&7

Both 3 and 7 are very lucky numbers. Three is special because of its importance in many religions. Over thousands of years vast numbers of people have worshiped what is called a Trinity, either three separate gods or one god in three forms.

Among Christians, the Trinity is the Father, the Son, and the Holy Ghost. Among the ancient Egyptians, it was Osiris, the Father; Isis, the Mother; and Horus, the Son, who together represented life.

Many say the number 7 is lucky because it was involved in the creation of the earth. As it is described in the Bible, it took God six days to create the heavens and the earth, and on the seventh day He finally rested.

The ancient Egyptians had another explanation. They believed the earth actually was a square four-sided house in which their three gods lived. As they saw it, four plus three—or seven—stood for a good life, which *is* lucky.

2&5

Many people have lucky numbers of their own. A girl in Princeton, New Jersey, named Elizabeth Owen Schwartz has two lucky numbers. One is 2. The other is 5.

The number 2 stands for her name. She arrived at it by using the table on the following page, in which each letter in the alphabet has its own number.

1 2 3 4 5 6 7 8 9
A B C D E F G H I
J K L M N O P Q R
S T U V W X Y Z

This is what she found.

ELIZABETH OWEN SCHWARTZ
5 3 9 8 1 2 5 2 8   6 5 5 5   1 3 8 5 1 9 2 8

Next she added up the twenty-one numbers involved, which came to 101. Then she dropped the zero, added the two 1's, and arrived at 2.

Her lucky number 5 stands for her birth date, which is November 14, 1960. Since November is the eleventh month, this became 11-14-1960, or $1 + 1 + 1 + 4 + 1 + 9 + 6 + 0$, which equals 23. She then added the 2 and the 3, which produced 5.

If all this is too much work, there is a simpler method. Eat an apple, count the seeds, and use the total as your lucky number.

Days and Holidays

Some days are better than others for being born, getting married, getting a haircut, and trimming your fingernails. The table below shows which days are recommended and which are not. If things might be different where you live, check with your local folklorist.

	BEING BORN	GETTING MARRIED	GETTING A HAIRCUT	TRIMMING YOUR FINGER-NAILS
MONDAY	Yes	Yes	Yes	Yes
TUESDAY	Yes	Yes	Yes	Yes
WEDNESDAY	Yes	Yes	Only sheep	No
THURSDAY	Yes	No	No	No
FRIDAY	No	No	No	No
SATURDAY	No	Yes	No	No
SUNDAY	Yes	Yes	No	No

73

Friday is the most miserable day of the week. If you try to get anything done, you will fail. Friday the thirteenth is even worse. But fortunately it occurs only once or twice a year.

If you have any doubts about how bad Friday is, remember it was on that day that Eve tempted Adam with an apple and they left the Garden of Eden, that Noah and his ark were engulfed by the great flood, and that Jesus was crucified.

New Year's Day is the most important day of the year. It affects all the other days to come. Therefore, it is sensible to take these steps:

At 12:01 A.M. make a dreadful commotion to frighten away any evil spirits; then eat a dish of pickled herring; then make sure a man walks all the way through your house. Then remember that the way you behave all day is the way you will behave all year. If you do these things, the year will be a good one.

Also, get somebody to kiss you. Otherwise, no one will for another year, which is a long time to wait.

Travel

If the bottom of one of your feet itches, you are going to take a trip. But do *not* leave on a Friday and do *not* use a black suitcase. When you do start, throw a pinch of salt over your left shoulder and twirl around three times on the balls of your feet, and you will have a safe journey.

If the first creature you meet after you set out is a blackbird, a cat, a chipmunk, a rabbit, a red-haired woman, or a snake, it is a bad sign.

If you step on your shadow or hear an owl hooting, it is equally bad.

In all such cases turn your hat around and pull your pockets out, or make a cross in the road, or spit.

If a cat crosses your path, also follow the directions on pages 100 and 101. If a red-haired woman does, make sure she gives you a pin.

If you do not take this advice, you can expect serious trouble.

If, for example, you step on a line, you will break your mother's spine.

Or if you step on a crack, you will break her back.

Or if you fall in a hole, you will break
her sugar bowl.

If you are traveling by car, it is a good time to make a wish. If you use these methods, your wish will come true.

When you cross a bridge, hold your breath until you reach the other side.

When you drive through a tunnel, put one hand on the ceiling and get the driver to honk the horn.

When you see a car with only one headlight on, smack your right fist with your left palm.

When you see a car with whitewall tires, stick a finger in your mouth. With your other hand, tap your forehead, then smack it hard.

Once you begin a journey, it is very bad luck
to turn back. But if you must, take these
precautions:

Follow another route home. If you are on foot,
take the first ten steps backward.

When you arrive, walk into your house backward.

Before you start out again, sit on the floor
and count to ten.

The Human Body

If you have a large, well-shaped nose, it is a
sign that you are noble, generous, and friendly.
   But if your nose itches, it is a sign that you
may have a fight,
   or kiss a fool,
   or cause people to gossip about you,
   or sneeze.

At one time sneezing was a serious problem. People believed that a person's soul, or spirit, was part of his breath and that he could sneeze his life away.

There also was another danger. If in sneezing he opened his mouth, evil spirits could enter his body. Or those already there could leave and attack others.

To prevent disaster the person nearest the sneezer would bless him. Which is why someone usually blesses you when you sneeze, even though he may not know the reason.

If one of your ears rings or burns or tingles or itches, it means that somebody is talking about you.

If is is your right ear, he is saying something good.

If it is your left ear, he is saying something bad.

If you want him to stop, you have two choices.

Repeat the name of every gossip you know. When you name the right one, your ear will stop ringing.

Or spit on one of your fingers, then rub it on the ear involved, and the gossip will bite his tongue.

The evil eye is a dreadful weapon. If you have it, you could harm or kill a person, an animal, or a plant with a single glance.

Children are among the easiest to harm with the evil eye. So are people who were just married and women about to have babies. But no one is safe.

Many people who have an evil eye are born with it. But others acquire one by getting drunk or looking through a knothole in a plank pried from an old wooden coffin.

Some who have this power say they did not know it until they harmed someone by accident. But others deliberately have used it to take revenge on those who anger them.

It is hard to tell who has an evil eye and who does not. But there are steps you can take to protect yourself against its influence if an enemy stares at you.

Stare back at him until he looks away.

Make a fist, stick your thumb between the first and second fingers, and point it in his direction.

Spit at him.

Suspend a holy medal from a strap around your head so that it hangs above your nose.

Draw large circles of mascara around your eyes.

Most people no longer believe in the evil eye. But those who have one know better.

If your upper lip itches, you will be kissed by someone who is tall. If your lower lip itches, you will be
kissed by someone who is short.

If you bite your tongue, you will tell a lie.

If you drink from a pool of dirty water, your teeth will fall out. But don't throw them away, for anyone who found them could control your every action. Instead, put them under your pillow. By morning they will have turned into coins.

If you yawn, be sure to cover your mouth. It will show what good manners you have. But it also will keep your soul from flying out or an evil spirit from jumping in, just as when you sneeze.

If you are faced with bad luck, it always is useful to spit. In ancient times people thought it was the most sensible thing to do, for saliva enabled them to digest their food, helped animals clean and heal their wounds, and looked like the fluid in which babies lived in their mothers' wombs—all of which seemed reason enough to rely on it for help.

If you cross your fingers, you will have good luck, avoid bad luck, and make your wishes come true. The reason for this, many say, is that Christ died on a cross.

There are at least two ways to cross your fingers properly. The most common involves placing the second finger of your right hand on top of the first finger in the form of an X. This is called a St. Andrew's Cross. It looks like this:

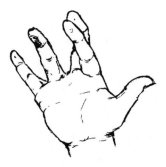

You also can use a Greek Cross. To form one, place the first finger of one hand on top of the knuckle of the first finger of the other. But make sure the fingers are at right angles.

If you make a wish, it is trapped where the fingers meet. Usually this is only for a brief time, but it always is long enough for the powers involved to do their work.

If you kiss your elbow,
you will turn
into a member
of the opposite sex.

Ailments and Cures

If you hang a string of onions in your house,
or wear a dime or a camphor ball around your neck,
or carry a potato with you,
or rub your feet with garlic,
or stand in the first rainfall in May,

you will be healthy.

If at any time you do get sick, the ancient Oriental charm, the Abracadabra, might help. But first you must write it on a sheepskin or a goatskin or a piece of parchment just as it is shown here.

```
A B R A C A D A B R A
A B R A C A D A B R
A B R A C A D A B
A B R A C A D A
A B R A C A D
A B R A C A
A B R A C
A B R A
A B R
A B
A
```

Then you must take it to a healer who deals in magic and have him read it aloud. And finally you must wear it around your neck on a string. If for some reason it does not work, there are, of course, all kinds of other remedies.

If you have stiff joints, you are in need of earthworm grease. Dig a dozen worms and simmer them in a skillet. Then pour off the worm oil as it collects and rub it into the stiffness.

If you have a stitch in your side or a crick in your neck, rub it gently with a flat stone. Then spit on the stone and put it back where you found it.

If you catch a cold, fry some onions, mix them with turpentine, and spread them on your chest. Or boil an old hog hoof and drink the water. Or kiss a mule on the nose.

If you have a sore throat, wrap a piece of bacon around your neck. Or use a dirty, sweaty sock a healthy friend has been wearing. If the foot of the sock covers the soreness in your throat, you will absorb his health and recover before you know it.

If you catch the chicken pox, lie on the floor of a chicken house and get somebody to chase a flock of hens over you.

If freckles cause you to suffer, wash your face in watermelon juice, or in buttermilk, or in the water a blacksmith has used to cool a hot horseshoe, or in dew, and you will wash them away.

If you use dew, do so before dawn on the first day of May. Wash your face seven times that morning and seven times on each of the next six mornings.

It also helps to rub ripe strawberries or cucumber slices on your freckles, or to cover them for a few minutes each day with mud or with cow manure. But cow manure tends to be itchy.

If you have warts, whirl a strip of bacon around your head until you get tired, then bury it, and when it rots they will disappear.

Or steal your mother's dishrag and bury it, and when it rots you will be cured.

Or rub each of your warts with a bean, a pickle, an onion, a potato slice, or the skin of a chicken gizzard, and bury it.

Or tie a knot in a string for each wart you have and bury it.

Or tie half a grapefruit over your warts and wear it all night, and sooner or later they will go away.

Or use rainwater that has collected in a tree stump.

As Tom Sawyer explained it, ". . . go all by yourself to the middle of the woods, where you know there's a spunk water stump, and just as it's midnight you stand back up against the stump and jam your hand in and say,

'Barley-corn, barley-corn, injun meal shorts,
Spunk-water, spunk-water, swaller these warts,'
and then walk away quick, eleven steps, with your eyes shut, and then turn around three times and walk home without speaking to anybody. . . ."

Or find a dead cat, and when the next moon shines take it to a cemetery and swing it around your head three times by the tail and bury it there. And you never again will have warts.

When none of this works, sometimes a wart witch can help, like the one this woman went to see for a wart on her lip when she was a girl in Texas.

". . . putting his left arm around my waist, he placed the forefinger of his right hand on top of that little seed wart and pressed hard, following the pressure with a circular massaging motion. I think I had my eyes closed from fright, but when I opened them . . . I was relieved to find his eyes were not on me at all. They had a far-far-away gaze. I wondered what he could see so far away. And he was mumbling. I couldn't make out one word, even though I held my breath to hear better. . . .

"Then he said, 'Young lady, don't put your hands on it; don't watch tha' thing grow. Fergit it. And you won't have a wart three weeks from now!' These were the last words I remember his saying to us.

"It took all the discipline I could exert to follow his instructions. . . . Never once did I look in the mirror directly at the wart. Never did I put my hands on it, though I would feel for it with the tip of my tongue. But eventually . . . I forgot my wart.

"Then one day it was gone! I examined my lip with the mirror . . . but there was no visible sign."

If you have hiccups, hold your nose, tilt your head back, and take a sip of water for each year you are old.

Or drink a glass of water from the far edge of a glass or through a napkin.

Or bring your little fingers as close together as you can without having them touch.

Or hold your breath and say "hiccup" nine times without hiccuping. And you won't.

If you want curly hair, pour rum or the juice of wild grapes on your head and eat bread crusts and carrots. But if you are a girl, don't whistle, or you also will grow a beard.

Animals, Birds, and Insects

If a black cat crosses your path, it means bad luck
unless you roll up your pants or hike up your skirts. . . .

or spit in your hat,
or spit in the road,
or cross your arms and fingers and toes,
or take nine steps backward,
or go home and start over.

It probably is hard to believe, but five thousand years ago ancient Egyptians worshiped cats. They also consulted them on many important matters which were decided by how a cat behaved—whether it sat down, for example, or stood up, or made a particular sound. When a cat died, it was preserved as a mummy and buried with kings and queens.

None of this should be too surprising, since cats are unusual creatures. They can see at night. Their eyes glow in the dark. They leap great distances without harming themselves. And they like nothing better than eating rats, which in those days plagued Egypt in great numbers.

Actually, black cats acquired their bad name only five hundred years ago. That was when people began to worry seriously about the Devil and demons and witches and other powers of the night.

As a result, no longer were they worshiped as goddesses. Instead they were feared as creatures who worked with the Devil and with witches in performing evil deeds. In fact, they still make people uneasy.

If you use the same pillow your dog uses,
you will dream what he dreams.

If you hold the hair of a horse in your hand, nothing can harm you. This also is true if you eat a chopped horsehair sandwich.

A horseshoe also will protect you. But it should be a shoe a horse lost and you found, and when you find it the prongs should be pointing toward you.

If it is to be helpful, you then must do one of two things.

Spit through the prongs, heave the shoe over your shoulder, and walk away without looking.

Or nail it above your front door with the prongs up so that the luck will not run out. Once the shoe is in place, everyone and everything in your home will be safe.

But what makes the horseshoe special has little to do with the horse.

For one thing, it contains iron, which once was regarded as a sacred metal that men could count on for protection. The Norse god of war, for example, wore iron gloves and used as a weapon an iron hammer which returned to him each time he threw it.

The shape of the shoe also resembles a crescent moon, which many early people counted on also for protection. In some countries church doors still are shaped like a crescent moon—or a horseshoe.

There also is a legend involving a blacksmith named Dunstan. It is said that the Devil came to Dunstan to have a hoof reshod and that the blacksmith tortured him until he agreed that neither he nor his helpers would ever enter a building protected by a horseshoe. Nor have they, as far as anyone knows.

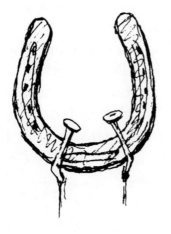

If you carry with you the foot of a rabbit, you will ward off bad luck and attract good luck.

There are two reasons for this. One is that the rabbit lives underground, yet survives despite the evil it encounters there. The other is that it produces a great number of children. Any animal which can do that must be lucky, it is said.

However, not just any rabbit's foot will do. To obtain the right kind, you must take these steps:

Shoot a rabbit with a silver bullet on a night when the moon is full.

Then cut off one of its hind feet. (In some places the right foot is better; in others it is the left.)

Then dip it in rainwater that has collected in a hollow stump.

For the foot to work properly, carry it in your left back pocket. If you don't have one, wear it around your neck. But don't lose it, for the older and drier it gets, the better it works.

If you manage to sprinkle salt on the tail of a bird, you will have good luck.

But this does not apply to owls. If one hoots or screeches or perches near your house, it means disaster is on its way. For the owl not only makes weird sounds and sees in the dark, it sees what the future holds.

You can stop its noise by wearing your clothes backward, or taking your shoes off and turning them upside down, or tying a knot in your pillowcase. But this will not keep you from disaster.

In ancient Greece no one feared the owl. It was the bird of the goddess Athena, who was concerned with good works and wisdom. But when in the night the owl hoots and screeches, it is not a good sound to hear.

If you pay attention, you will find that there are fewer blue jays and other jaybirds around on weekends than during the week.

Each Friday most jaybirds go to hell to help the Devil. They report all the miserable things people have done that week. They also bring him twigs to keep his fires burning. This old song describes it:

> Don't you hear that blue jay call?
> Don't you hear them dead sticks fall?
> He's a throwin' down the firewood
>   for we-all
> All on a Friday morning.

The few jaybirds you do see on weekends still are checking on you and your neighbors. So watch out.

If the first robin you see in the spring flies up, you
will have good luck for the rest of the year. But if it
flies down,

you won't.

If a fly lands on your nose, somebody has something to tell you.

But if it is a dragonfly or a darning needle, as they are called, cover your mouth and your nose, or it will sew them up. Also cover your ears, for it will fly into one and out the other.

If a cricket moves in with you, your home will be a happy one. But if it leaves, trouble is on the way. If you kill one, also watch out. Its relatives will eat all your clothes and the curtains and the rugs.

If a spider swings down
in front of you,
you will hear good news
or you will have good luck.
If you walk into
a spider's web,
you will get a letter
or meet a friend.
If you find
one of your initials
in the threads of a web,
you will be lucky forever.
But if a spider crawls
toward you,
you will have a quarrel.
And if you step on one
and kill it,
you will be very poor
for the rest of your life.

Plants

If you catch a falling leaf, you will
have a good and happy life.

If you find a four-leaf clover, you also will find good luck. If you wear it inside your shoe, your luck will be even better.

But if you brag about your luck, knock on wood, or you will lose it. For best results, knock three times.

People have been knocking on wood for thousands of years to protect their good luck. At one time they hoped the noise would keep evil spirits from hearing about it and taking it from them. Some even knocked on trees to get the tree gods to protect them.

Of course, few of us believe in tree gods or evil spirits. But we still knock on wood.

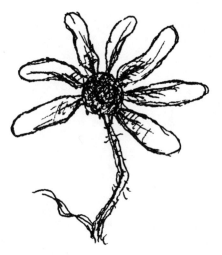

If you have questions about the future, a daisy often can answer them.

Pull off its petals one by one. When you remove the first, say "yes"; the second, "no"; the third, "maybe so." Continue this way until you have one petal left. It will have the answer you are seeking.

For some questions you will need a dandelion that has gone to seed. The number of puffs it takes to blow the seeds away will tell you the following:

The time. (Each puff equals one hour.)

Whether your mother wants you. (If all the seeds fly off at once, she does.)

When you will be punished next. (Depending on your previous record, each puff equals an hour, a day, a week, a month, or a year.)

If at Christmas you stand under a sprig of mistletoe and nobody kisses you, you have every right to be disappointed. For there is nothing more powerful in attracting affection than this plant.

Because it grows on trees and never touches the ground, many ancient people regarded the mistletoe as sacred. In one group priests in white robes harvested the plant with a golden sickle which also never touched the ground.

Then the people would hang it above their doorways to welcome guests, which led to this business of kissing.

There is probably nothing more useful than the root of the mandrake plant. It will protect your health, increase your wealth, make you attractive to the opposite sex, and keep away evil spirits.

Split down the middle like two hairy legs, it looks like a human being and in some ways behaves like one.

But it is not easy to obtain. The genuine mandrake grows only around the Mediterranean Sea and in the Himalaya Mountains in central Asia.° In addition, it can be removed from the ground during only two periods of the year: in late June and in late December when the sun is farthest from the earth. And it must be done at night in the light of a full moon.

What complicates things further is the plant's behavior. It shrieks when it is pulled from the ground. And its shriek is so loud it will split an eardrum and so dreadful it will drive a person mad, or kill him.

To obtain a mandrake root, first obtain the following: a strong, hungry black dog with a stout collar; a strong black cord at least thirty feet long; a large, raw beefsteak; and a large quantity of soft wax.

Then carefully follow these directions:

1. As protection against the shriek, plug your ears and your dog's ears with wax.

° It has a relative in the United States called the mayapple which does not have its power.

2. Loosen the soil around the plant.

3. Tie one end of the cord to the root and the other end to the dog's collar.

4. Drop the steak just beyond the dog's reach.

When he lunges for the steak, he will yank out the mandrake. And you will have your prize, if you have used enough wax.

If you are a farmer, you probably know that vegetables that grow underground should be planted at night when there is no moon. Otherwise, they will rise to the surface and get sunburned.

What you may not know is that potatoes and onions should be planted together. At least that is what a farmer in Maine advises. It is a great convenience, he says, for the onions irritate the eyes of the potatoes and produce tears, which does away with the need for watering.

The Weather

At noon on February 2 the groundhog awakens from its winter's sleep and crawls out of its nest in the ground.

If it is a sunny day and it sees its shadow, it dives back into its hole in fright and sleeps for six weeks more, which means six weeks more of winter. If it is a cloudy day, it goes about its business, which means spring is on the way.

But there also are other signs you need to know.

If there is a ring around the moon, expect bad weather. The number of stars inside the ring will tell you how long it will last.

If a new moon is tipped on end, expect rain, for the rain it has collected between its points will pour out.

Also expect rain if your cat sneezes or yawns or licks its tail,

or if your dog eats grass or scratches wildly,

or if you step on an ant,

or if your nose won't stop itching,

or if you dream of eating grapes.

Expect cold, snowy weather if the robins seem friend-
lier than usual,
  or the wasps and hornets build their nests higher,
  or the hogs are fatter,
  or other animals have more fur,
  or the oaks are thick with acorns and the squirrels are
busy hiding them.
  How cold it will be depends on how warm it was during the summer. There will be as many freezing days as
there were sunny days.
  How much snow there will be depends on when the
first snow falls. If it falls on the thirtieth day of the
month, there will be thirty days of snow. If it falls on
the first day, there will be one.

  If you want to be sure the weather will be clear on
a particular day, eat everything clear off the table the
night before.

Death

Before a death occurs, there is a warning.

If a dog howls or lies on its back with
its paws in the air,
or an owl screeches or a whippoorwill calls,
or a picture drops from the wall without
any apparent cause,
or there is a rapping or a knocking sound
for which there is no reason,
or you hear in one of your ears a ringing
like the tolling of church bells,
or you see a falling star,
or you dream of muddy water,
someone nearby or someone you know will
die soon.

If a person who dies kept bees, it is important to let them know he is dead. Stand in front of the hive and say, "Your master has died." If this is not done, they also will die, or they will leave.

If you see a funeral procession, it is bad luck. If you count the number of cars, it is even worse. For each one you count takes a year from your life.

If you pass a graveyard and do not hold your breath, you will die very soon.

If you point at a grave, your finger will rot away unless you stick it in the ground.

If you count one hundred stars, you will die as you count the last one.

If you suddenly shiver, someone or something is walking where your grave will be.

Each person who dies as a result of violence, or with a secret, or with unfinished business will return to earth as a ghost to settle his affairs so that he may rest in peace.

If you feel a breath of cold air or hear strange sounds, or a door opens for no reason, or you see lights moving in a cemetery, a ghost may be nearby.

Animals also return as ghosts. Pigs, white foxes, giant dogs, headless bulls, and other creatures all roam silently through the countryside on missions known only to themselves.

In Bunker, Missouri, for example, they tell of a giant ghost dog that a doctor named J. Gordon encountered years ago. Here is what happened, as it was described to the folklorist Vance Randolph.

"Crossing a little stream on horseback, near the Bay Cemetery about nine miles west of Bunker, late at night, [Dr. Gordon] saw a figure like a dog, but very much larger. The thing apparently walked on the water without a sound or a ripple. [He] saw it many times, once in the bright moonlight. Sometimes it crossed ahead of him.

"One time it jumped on the horse [just] behind the doctor. The animal plunged wildly and the doctor fired his Derringer into the ghost twice, but it was not dislodged.° He struck at the beast with his fist, but could

° A Derringer is a pocket pistol with a short barrel.

feel nothing, and his arm slashed right through the figure as if nothing were there."

There are many such tales.

If you meet the ghost of a human being, the best thing to do is gather your courage and speak to it. Say, "What in the name of the Lord do you want?" and it will explain or disappear.

The Moon and the Stars

To learn the future, find yourself an astrologer. Just as those in ancient Babylon did, he will study his maps, charts, and tables and tell you a great many things.

To do so he must know precisely when and where you were born. Then, through a complicated system four thousand years old, he will find where the sun, the moon, the constellations, and the planets were at that time. For it was their position that decided your destiny.

His most important information will come from the zodiac, an imaginary circular zone through which the major heavenly bodies move.* Each of its twelve sections has its own constellation, or sign. One of these is the sign under which you were born, which affects your life in many ways.

When your astrologer finishes his calculations, he will "cast" a horoscope which describes your future.

But if there is no astrologer available, you still can get an idea of the kind of person you will become. Just look below under the right sign.

 January 21–February 19: Aquarius, the Water Bearer. Intelligent, idealistic, emotional, unpredictable.

 February 20–March 20: Pisces, the Fish. Gentle, loving, peaceful, filled with good intentions.

 March 21–April 20: Aries, the Ram. Adventurous, courageous, lively, impatient.

 April 21–May 22: Taurus, the Bull. Loyal, loving, practical, artistic.

---

* The sun actually does not move. Nor do the stars, which are more distant suns. The movement of the earth makes them seem to move.

May 23–June 21: Gemini, the Twins. Cheerful, lively, but at times jumpy.

 June 22–July 22: Cancer, the Crab. Hardworking and loyal, but a worrywart.

 July 23–August 22: Leo, the Lion. Brave, generous, a leader, but at times bossy.

 August 23–September 23: Virgo, the Virgin. Careful and orderly, a thinker, but overly critical.

 September 24–October 21: Libra, the Scales. Pleasant, kind, gentle, dignified, artistic.

 October 22–November 21: Scorpio, the Scorpion. Honest, intelligent, hard-working, usually successful.

 November 22–December 20: Sagittarius, the Archer. Friendly, generous, helpful, usually successful.

 December 21–January 20: Capricorn, the Goat. Serious, ambitious, dignified, honorable.

If you see the new moon
over your left shoulder,
and it is the first time
you have seen it,
and you have in your pocket
a silver coin,
turn it over
and make a wish,
and it will come true.

Or wish on the first star you see tonight,
and when you do, use this old rhyme.

> Star light, star bright,
> The first star I see tonight,
> I wish I may, I wish I might,
> Get the wish I wish tonight.

And you will.

Notes
Sources and Related Beliefs
Bibliography

Abbreviations

CFQ   *California Folklore Quarterly*

HF   *Hoosier Folklore*

JA   Louis C. Jones Archives, New York State Historical Associa-
tion, Cooperstown, N.Y. Folklore collected in the 1940s at
Albany State Teachers College, Albany, N.Y., now Albany
State College, under the direction of Professor Louis C. Jones.

JAF   *Journal of American Folklore*

KFR   *Kentucky Folklore Record*

MAFS   Memoirs of the American Folklore Society

MF   *Midwest Folklore*

NCF   *North Carolina Folklore*

NYFQ   *New York Folklore Quarterly*

RU   Material from the author's folklore collection contributed
since 1963 by his students at Rutgers University.

SFQ   *Southern Folklore Quarterly*

TA   Harold W. Thompson Archives, New York State Historical
Association, Cooperstown, N.Y. Folklore collected in the
1940s and 1950s by Cornell University students under the
direction of Professor Harold W. Thompson.

TFSB   *Tennessee Folklore Society Bulletin*

TXFS   Texas Folklore Society publication

UM   Maryland Folklore Archives, University of Maryland, College
Park, Md. Including folklore collected by students in the
1960s and 1970s.

WF   *Western Folklore*

Notes

The publications cited are described in the bibliography.

Good lucks and bad lucks (p. 11): To better understand the beliefs in this book there are a number of terms you should know.

A *folk belief* is an approach to dealing with the problems of everyday life. Ordinarily it has no basis in fact, but many members of a group accept it to one degree or another or at least do not object to it. At one time this was the case with all the beliefs in this book. When somebody believes so strongly in one of these ideas that his behavior is affected, it is not only a folk belief but a *superstition*. This is the case, for example, when he will not walk under a ladder or avoids contact with the number 13 or stays home when his nose itches because, according to the old belief, it means company is coming.

A *charm* is a technique which produces good luck through the use of words or gestures. The "star bright" rhyme (p. 133) and the Abracadabra cure (p. 90) are charms. So are crossing your fingers and spitting in your hat.

An *amulet* is an object you carry with you or hang on a wall as protection against bad luck. A wolf's eye, a stone with a hole in it, and a horseshoe all are said to be useful.

A *talisman* is an object which attracts good luck, such as a four-leaf clover or a rabbit's foot. A *mascot* is a stuffed animal, a doll, or a similar talisman.

Divination is a ritual to determine what the future holds. See those relating to love (p. 20) and children (p. 28).

A *sign* is an event which foretells the future, such as those that

135

predict the weather (pp. 120–122). An *omen* is a sign that promises bad luck: a screeching owl, for example.

A *taboo* is a rule, usually not written down, which forbids a particular act, such as sleeping on a table or starting a trip on a Friday. If the rule is ignored, it is said, bad luck will result.

A *counteractant* is a method of turning away evil or changing your luck. Spitting, pulling your pockets out, and turning a hat around are common techniques.

As noted in the text, all this depends on the use of magic, through which we give things power they otherwise would not have. Frequently we use *imitative magic,* which is based on the idea that one thing can affect another if they are similar. Thus, if you carry a baby upstairs before you carry him downstairs, he will rise in the world (p. 27). Or if you have money in your pockets on New Year's Day, they will contain money all year. We also use *contagious magic,* which is based on the idea that things that have been in contact can affect one another after they separate. This is the case with the love potions on page 16 and the "rotting cures" for warts on page 95.

Apples (p. 17): In American folklore apples are associated primarily with pie, cider, and love. In England they also are associated with beauty, or at least with face creams. In one sixteenth-century recipe mashed apples are mixed with hog grease and rosewater. In another they are cooked with bread crumbs, crushed almonds, and equal quantities of white wine, rosewater, and soap. See Jagendorf, *NYFQ* 18.

Witches (p. 51): For almost four hundred years, starting in the fourteenth century, the Christian church waged a vigorous attack against witchcraft and other pagan practices. In Europe hundreds of thousands of persons believed to be witches or warlocks were burned, hanged, or drowned. In the Massachusetts Bay Colony, where witch-hunts in America centered, hundreds of persons were jailed, and in Salem nineteen were executed in 1692.

Usually the victims were harmless old men and women who sold folk cures or good luck charms, or who tried to use spells to forecast the future, or who were merely eccentric.

When the accused would not confess to witchcraft or was not convicted in a court, local people often took matters into their own hands and conducted a "trial by water." The suspect was cast into a deep river or lake. If he returned to the surface, he was declared guilty and was drowned. Only if he drowned on his own was he regarded as innocent.

Whistling (p. 61): Actors, coal miners, and sailors traditionally have regarded whistling on the job as an invitation to disaster. Scholars say this fear is an ancient one. Primitive man assumed that evil spirits were responsible for all sounds he could not account for, including the whistling of the wind. He felt that if he whistled, an evil spirit might respond, which would not have been helpful.

Numbers (p. 69): Although many people regard the number 13 as unlucky, the United States government does not. If you closely examine the back of a dollar bill, you will find a partially completed pyramid with thirteen steps and an eagle with thirteen arrows in one talon and an olive branch with thirteen leaves and thirteen berries in the other, all of which represent the original thirteen colonies.

Onions and garlic (p. 89): On the pyramid of Cheops in Egypt there are carved an onion and a garlic bulb, which seems only right since for thousands of years man used these plants to protect his health. He strung them like beads on a necklace and hung them in his home, carried them in his pockets, ate them raw, drank their juice, spread them fried, boiled, or raw on his chest, and rubbed them on his feet. In some respects he was right. In recent years we have learned that both onions and garlic have ingredients that are useful in treating various ailments. See E. Wilson, WF 12.

Warts (p. 95): Warts are rather mysterious growths on the skin that frequently come and go for no apparent reason. Most result either from a virus infection or from a case of nerves. But not too long ago it generally was believed that one "caught" warts by handling toads, which looked as if they already had them. Over the years victims and sympathizers developed countless "cures," most of which depended on magic rituals. Curiously, some seemed to work. One probable reason was that the ritual gave the victim hope, which soothed his nerves. But time also was involved. Some cures required weeks, even months, to take effect. And since warts come and go, many went before the time was up.

Hiccups (p. 98): In case you were not sure, a hiccup is an "involuntary spasmodic contraction of the diaphragm followed by sudden closure of the glottis," which is the opening between the vocal cords. This closure blocks the passage of air which in turn causes that funny sound. People have developed countless cures for hiccups. But some physicians say the most effective remedy for a run-of-the-mill case is exhaling carbon dioxide into a paper bag, then repeatedly rebreathing it. This helps to restore a more normal rhythm in breathing. See *The Columbia Encyclopedia*, p. 946.

Telling the bees (p. 124): At one time people in Europe and in New England believed that bees were as intelligent as human beings. As a result, if they owned bees, they informed them of important events within the family. If someone was married, for example, a piece of wedding cake was placed in front of a hive or a white ribbon was hung from it. If someone died, a black ribbon was used. If it was their keeper, a member of the family stood in front of the hive and told the bees. If this was not done, it was feared they would die or leave. The New England poet John Greenleaf Whittier described this custom in 1858 in his poem "Telling the Bees." He concluded,

"Stay at home, pretty bees, fly not hence!
Mistress Mary is dead and gone!"

Sources and Related Beliefs

Representative sources are given for each belief, along with significant variants. If an item appears to be nationwide or worldwide, the term "general" is used. If an item is numbered in a published source, the number is given in parentheses following the citation. Each publication cited is described in the bibliography.

p. 11 *Good Lucks and Bad Lucks:* Maryland—A term reported by Mary Bayles, UM, 1970.

Love and Marriage

p. 15 *Pull a hair:* General.
p. 16 **Love potions.** *Blood:* New York—JA, 1945; North Carolina—Hand (4232); Nova Scotia—Creighton (61). VARIANTS: General—Blood is added to tomato soup, vegetable soup, or spaghetti sauce, or smeared on candy or apples. *Fingernails, toenails:* Pennsylvania—Belmont School, Philadelphia, 1971. VARIANTS: General—Other beverages range from cider to whiskey. *Pop knuckle:* New York—Reported by Mary Glus, JA, 1945.
p. 17 **Whether you will marry.** *Apple:* New York—TA, 1940s. *Moustache, pie point, cat's tail:* New York—JA, 1945. *Stumble:* Maryland—UM, 1969. VARIANT: General—Stub toe/See beau/Touch blue/Come true. *Hairy legs:*

Maine—The author learned this as a student at Colby College, Waterville, late 1940s. VARIANT: Illinois— Girls with hairy legs acquire rich husbands, Hyatt (9324). M: Louisiana—Roberts, JAF 40 (116). VARIANT: Illinois—A spider web is the medium, Hyatt (9090). Bath: New Jersey—Churchill Junior High School, East Brunswick, 1972; New York—P. Allen, NYFQ 5. VARIANT: North Carolina—It is bad luck to take one the day you marry, Hand (4756). Table: General.

p. 18 **You will dream.** Mirror: Turner, TXFS 13. VARIANTS: General—Few involve a dream. One method calls for walking backward up a flight of stairs while looking into a mirror to see your future mate. Nine stars: General. Nightgown: New Jersey—Valley Road School, Princeton, 1973. Bed posts: Maryland—UM, 1970. Shoelace: New York—Reported by Boyd M. Swem, JA, 1943.

p. 19 *If you fill.* Maryland—UM, 1969. VARIANT: Louisiana— Only one trip is required, Roberts, JAF 40 (133).

p. 20 *Write your name.* New York—The author's childhood recollection, Brooklyn, 1930s. VARIANTS: General—The simplest is an Ozark Mountains version in which one calls "False, true, false, true," in sequence while crossing out matching letters, Randolph, JAF 46.

p. 21 *Gizzards.* New Jersey—RU, 1972; Tennessee—Farr, SFQ 2.

p. 23, 24 **Wedding customs:** General.

Children

p. 25 *Forehead:* General. *Palm:* Maryland—UM, 1970; North Carolina—Hand (131). *Dandelion:* General. *Apple:* New York—Childhood recollection, Delmar, 1930s, Barbara Carmer Schwartz, Princeton, N.J.; Louisiana —Roberts, JAF 40; Alabama—Browne (3050). *Triplets:* New Jersey—RU, 1971; Texas—Hendricks, WF 24.

p. 26 **Physical characteristics.** New York—TA, 1940s; JA, 1945.

p. 27 *To help rise:* Tennessee—Farr, *JAF* 52 (1); Kansas—Koch, p. 81. *Fingernails:* Colorado—Davidson, *WF* 13 (7); Kentucky—Pope, *KFR* 11; New York—TA, 1940s. *Onions:* General. VARIANTS: General—Garlic; New York—A silk bag is used to hold the pieces, McCadden, *NYFQ* 3. See discussion "Onions and garlic" in Notes. *Hard-hearted:* Maine—Overheard in grocery, Deer Isle, 1973; Ozark Mountains—Randolph, p. 208.

p. 28 *Future:* General.

The Household

p. 29 *In one door:* Kentucky—Pope, *KFR* 11. *Closet:* New York—TA, 1940s. *Doorknob:* General. *Hop downstairs:* New York—The author's childhood recollection, 1930s, Brooklyn; Alabama—Browne (2274). *Run around your house:* New Jersey—Princeton High School, Princeton, 1973.

p. 30 *Ax and knife:* Pennsylvania—Belmont School, Philadelphia, 1971; Illinois—Hyatt (12592). VARIANTS: General—Fights nightmares; cuts fever, chills. *Get out of bed:* General.

p. 31 *Sleep on a table.* New Jersey—Churchill Junior High School, East Brunswick, 1972; American students in Tokyo—Simon, *WF* 12. *Spin a chair:* Colorado—Davidson, *WF* 13; Alabama—Browne (2303). *Friendship will end:* New York—TA, 1940s.

p. 32 *Break a mirror:* General. *Wait seven hours:* New Jersey—Churchill Junior High School, East Brunswick, 1972. *Swiftly moving river:* Tennessee—Page, *TFSB* 20. *Graveyard:* New York—TA, 1940s.

p. 33 *Ladder:* General.

p. 34 *Find a pin:* General. *If points away:* Frazier, *TFSB* 2.

p. 35 **Moving.** *Broom:* Indiana—Dundes, *MF* 11 (123); Kentucky—Thomas (1588). *Cat:* Tennessee—Hatcher, *SFQ* 19; California—Dresslar, p. 35. *Pig trough:* Alabama—Browne (2269); New York—TA, 1940s. *Friday:*

Kentucky—Pope, *KFR* 11; Tennessee—Hatcher, *SFQ* 19; Indiana—Tullis, *HF* 5.

Food and Drink

p. 36 *First and fourth fingers:* Kentucky—Fowler, *SFQ* 14. VARI- ANT: General—One who can bring these fingers to- gether will marry.

p. 37 *Wishbone:* General. VARIANTS: Kentucky—The loser need not tell his wish, but he will marry first, Fowler, *SFQ* 14; Indiana—The person with the shortest piece wins. It then is placed over the front door; its owner will marry the first person of the opposite sex to enter, Dundes, *MF* 11 (74).

p. 38 *If you eat peas:* General. *Cabbage:* Maryland—UM, 1970.

p. 39 *Salt:* General.

p. 40 *Banana:* New Jersey—RU, 1972; Louisiana—Hand (7953).

p. 41 *Kiss the cook:* New York—Childhood recollection, Delmar, 1930s, Barbara Carmer Schwartz, Princeton, N.J.; North Carolina—Hand (2862); Illinois—Hyatt (7749).

Clothing

p. 42 *Butterfly lands:* Texas—Turner, TXFS 13; Tennessee— Hatcher, *SFQ* 19. *Bite off its head:* Texas—Turner, TXFS 13; North Carolina—Hand (3165). VARIANTS: California—Bite off the tail, Hendricks, *WF* 24; Ozark Mountains—Crush body between teeth, Randolph, *JAF* 46. *Hem:* Texas—Turner, TXFS 13. VARIANT: Alabama—If the hem of your dress turns up, you will get kicked, Browne (2618).

p. 43 *Throw a shoe:* Illinois—The author learned this while he was a student at Northwestern University, 1950s; Hyatt (10668). *Shoelace:* New Jersey—RU, 1971. VARI- ANTS: These involve shoelaces that become untied. Alabama—Mark a cross on ground, place the shoe on the cross, and retie the shoelace, Woodall, *JAF* 43. Ozark Mountains—If a shoelace becomes untied, get

a friend to retie it, Randolph, *JAF* 46. *One shoe off:*
Turner, TXFS 13. *A year of trouble:* JA, 1945.

p. 44 *Right sock, right shoe:* General. *Backward:* General. *Under-*
wear: New York—J. R. Foster, *NYFQ* 13 (28).

p. 45 *Hat and pockets:* General.

Friends and Neighbors

p. 46 *If you drop a knife . . . sneeze:* General. *Glass of water:*
Ozark Mountains—Randolph, *JAF* 46. VARIANT: Ten-
nessee—According to this old rhyme, company is
coming if your nose itches: "Peaches, peaches, my
nose itches/Somebody's coming/With a hole in their
breeches!" Page, *TFSB* 20; Hatcher, *SFQ* 19.

p. 47 *A dirty, greasy dishrag:* Iowa—Hines, *WF* 24 (183); Texas
—Turner, TXFS 13; Indiana—Tullis, *HF* 5; Ozark
Mountains—Randolph, *JAF* 40. *Stays too long:* North
Carolina—Hand (3901, 3902). VARIANT: Southern
United States—If you don't want a visitor, drop the
dishrag in molasses, Puckett, p. 439.

p. 48 *If you and a friend:* New York—Reported by Barbara C.
Davenport, JA, 1945.

p. 49 *Two of you wash:* Alabama—Browne (2573, 2574). *Or dry:*
New York—Reported by Dawn Koert, JA, 1945.

p. 50 *Bread and butter:* General. VARIANT: Texas—"Bread and
butter, come to supper," Turner, TXFS 13. This involves the use of imitative magic. Since "bread and
butter" stick together and "salt and pepper" go together, the persons who recite either will not be
separated again. *Time to go home:* New York—The
author's childhood recollection, Brooklyn, 1930s; Illinois—Hyatt (14199).

Witches

p. 51 *Four joints:* Illinois—Hyatt (15853). *Broom:* Kentucky—
Thomas, p. 282; Pope, *KFR* 11. VARIANT: General—A

broom straw is used rather than a broom. *Scissors:*
Maryland—UM, 1970.

p. 52 *Crawl up a wall:* New Jersey—RU, 1971.

p. 53, 54 **Witches:** General.

p. 55 *Cat's bone:* Texas—Turner, TXFS 13; Ozark Mountains—
Randolph, JAF 46; Illinois—Hyatt (15865–7). *Magic
mirrors:* Ozark Mountains—Randolph, JAF 46. Such
mirrors are framed on only three sides.

p. 56 *The Lord's Prayer:* Ozark Mountains—Randolph, p. 265.
Hand on heel: General—Jennings, p. 97; Alabama—
Browne (3300); North Carolina—Hand (5585). *Black
cat:* Ohio—Adaptation of nineteenth-century ritual,
Miller, JAF 57. VARIANTS: North Carolina—To become
a witch eat crickets or grasshoppers, Hand (5594);
Kentucky—At sunrise stand atop a mountain, curse
God, swear loyalty to the Devil, and shoot a silver
bullet through a white handkerchief which, if every-
thing is done properly, will bleed, Combs, JAF 27.

p. 57 **Protection against harm.** *A circle:* New Jersey—John
Witherspoon School, Princeton, 1972. *Spit in your hat:*
General. *Wolf's eye:* Pennsylvania—Belmont School,
Philadelphia, 1971. *Triangle:* Ozark Mountains—Ran-
dolph, JAF 46. *Horseshoe:* General. *To break the spell:*
Pennsylvania—Belmont School, Philadelphia, 1971;
Illinois—Hyatt (16352).

School

p. 58 *Sleep with a school book:* General. *Kiss it:* Kentucky—
Thomas (89). VARIANT: Texas—Stamp on the book
with your foot, Turner, TXFS 13.

p. 59 **Taking a test:** *Don't shave:* New York—TA, 1940s, Cornell
University. *Inside out, backward:* General. See p. 44.
Charms: General. See discussion "Good lucks and
bad lucks" in Notes. *Step on every crack:* New York—
A childhood practice of the author, Brooklyn, 1930s.
Use the same pen: New York—TA, 1940s. *Or a new
one:* England—Opie, p. 227. *Same desk:* New York—

TA, 1940s. *Cross your legs:* New York— TA, 1940s; England—Opie, p. 227.

p. 60 *Swallow a goldfish:* Arizona—Simon, *WF* 12.

Work

p. 61 *If an actor whistles:* New York—Reported by Loretta Klee, TA, 1946, Chemung County. VARIANT: General—He will whistle himself out of a job. See discussion "Whistling" in Notes. *Wish good luck:* Maryland—Reported by Julia C. Fitch, UM, 1970; California—The appropriate thing to say is "Go out and break a leg," Gross, *WF* 20. *Fresh flowers, rocking chair, peacock, yellow costume:* General. *Shoes squeak:* New York— TA, 1940s.

p. 62 *Basketball:* Maryland—Reported by Gail Kizmer, UM, 1970. **Baseball.** *Wears gum:* New York—TA, 1940s. *Taps bat, changes bats:* New York—JA, 1945. *Bats crossed:* Colorado—Davidson, *WF* 13. *Prize fighter:* American students in Tokyo—Simon, *WF* 12. *Racing driver:* New Mexico—Penrod, *WF* 27.

p. 63 **Fishing.** *Pig:* Illinois—Author learned as a student at Northwestern University, 1950s. *Fiddle:* Maine—Various fishermen, Deer Isle, in line with a belief that music attracts fish.

p. 64 *Cornerstone:* General.

p. 65 **Sailor.** *Friday, name changed, corpse:* General in New England seafaring communities. *Map, bucket:* New York —TA, 1940s. *Whistle up a storm:* General. See discussion "Whistling" in Notes. *Child:* New York—Reported by Loretta Klee, TA, 1946, Chemung County.

Money

p. 66 *Eyebrows:* Texas—Turner, TXFS 13. *Hairy arms:* New York—TA, 1940s. *Mole:* General. *Palm itches:* General. VARIANTS: Indiana—You are going to shake hands with someone, Dundes, *MF* 11 (62); New York—You

145

are going to meet someone, JA, 1945. *Pocket:* General. *Scratch it:* Texas—Turner, TXFS 13. VARIANT: California—If the right hand itches, you will receive money; if the left hand itches, you will spend money, *The Golden Era* XII (Feb. 12, 1865), p. 2, as quoted in Mills, *WF* 11.

p. 67 *Shooting star:* General. *Bury a coin:* New York—A practice among children in the Flatbush section of Brooklyn, 1930s. *Wear a dime:* Illinois—Hyatt (13218); Maryland—UM, 1970. *Bubbles:* New York—General. VARIANTS: General—Coffee, cocoa, tea, soda pop; Maryland—Wrap coffee bubbles in paper, carry in pocket for good luck, TA, 1946. *Honeybee:* Ozark Mountains—Randolph, *JAF* 46. *Spider:* England—The spider is called a money spider, Opie, p. 219. *Horses:* North Carolina—Hand (3415). VARIANT: Oregon—For the same result, "stamp one white horse" one hundred times. To do so, wet tip of one finger, touch it to palm of opposite hand, Hines, *WF* 24 (121). In some areas "stamping a white horse" is a technique in wishing for anything, not only money. *Clear water:* Illinois—Hyatt (7331). *Fish:* Ozark Mountains—Randolph, *JAF* 46.

p. 68 *Spit:* New England—Johnson, p. 72.

Numbers

p. 69, 70, 71, 72 *13, 3 & 7:* General. *2 & 5:* General—The "lucky number" techniques are recorded in various archives in the United States. Brown reports them in England, p. 44. *Apple:* Maryland—UM, 1970.

Days and Holidays

p. 73 *Some days are better:* Based on a survey of regional collections. *Only sheep:* New York—TA, 1946.

p. 74 *Friday:* General. **New Year's Day.** *Evil Spirits:* General. *Pickled herring, man walks:* Maryland—UM, 1970.

VARIANTS: General—It is best if the man is dark, is married, and comes bearing food. North Carolina—A red-haired man is best, Hand (3888); a woman means bad luck, Hand (3890). *Behavior:* New York—Reported by Mary Tessier, JA, 1945. *Kissing:* Illinois—The author learned this belief as a student at Northwestern University, 1950s.

Travel

p. 75 *If your foot itches:* General. VARIANTS: Indiana—If the bottom of your right foot itches you will travel, Dundes, *MF* 11; Texas—If it is the left foot you will go where you are not wanted, Turner, TXFS 13. *Friday:* General. *Suitcase:* Maine—Beck, p. 68. *Salt:* Tennessee—Farr, *JAF* 48; New York—TA, 1940s. *Twirl:* Illinois—Hyatt (12807).

p. 76 *Blackbird:* New York—TA, 1940s. *Cat, rabbit:* Tennessee—Hatcher, *SFQ* 19. *Chipmunk:* Maine—Beck, p. 68. *Red-haired woman:* Illinois—Wine, *MF* 7 (85). *Snake:* Maryland—UM, 1970. *Shadow:* New York—J. R. Foster, *NYFQ* 13. *Owl:* General. *Hat, pockets:* Tennessee—Hatcher, *SFQ* 19. *Cross:* General. *Spit:* North Carolina—Hand (3791). *Pin:* North Carolina—Hand (3790). *Mother's spine, back:* General. VARIANTS: General—Grandmother's spine, Devil's spine or back. Ozark Mountains—Put your foot onto a crack/ And you will bust your mother's back, Randolph, *JAF* 46. New York—If you step on a crack, a bear will eat you, reported by Jean Tracy, JA, 1945.

p. 77 *Sugar bowl:* California—Simon, *WF* 12.

p. 78 *Bridge:* Indiana—Davidson, *WF* 16. VARIANTS: New York—A covered bridge is required, Beckwith, *JAF* 36; JA, 1945; Texas—There is no need to cross a bridge, just spit on it, Turner, TXFS 13. *Tunnel:* Kansas—Davidson, *WF* 13. *Headlight:* Kansas—Davidson, *WF* 13. *Whitewall tires:* New York—Reported by Irene Pastore, JA, 1945.

p. 79 *Turn back:* General. *Another route:* Illinois—Hyatt (13017). *Ten steps:* Ozark Mountains—Randolph, *JAF* 46. *Backward:* Alabama—Browne (154). *Count to ten:* Indiana—Dundes, *MF* 11; Illinois—Wine, *MF* 7; New York—Gardner, p. 300.

The Human Body

p. 80 **Nose.** *Noble:* New York—TA, 1940s. *Fight:* Oklahoma—Simon, *WF* 12. *Fool:* Minnesota—Hines, *WF* 24 (17). *Gossip:* Kansas—Hines, *WF* 24 (22). See reference to itching nose in sources for p. 46.

p. 81 *Sneezing:* General.

p. 82 *Ears:* Kentucky—Pope, *KFR* 11; Colorado—Hines, *WF* 24 (4); Indiana—Dundes, *MF* 11 (60); California—*The Golden Era* XII (Feb. 12, 1865), p. 2, as quoted in Mills, *WF* 11; Maryland—UM, 1970; New York—TA, 1940s.

p. 83, 84 *Evil eye:* General. *Holy medal:* Christian Syrian-Lebanese communities in the United States, Canada—Naff, *JAF* 78.

p. 85 *Lip itches:* Maryland—UM, 1970.

p. 86 *Bite your tongue:* New York—Learned by author during his childhood, Brooklyn, 1930s. *Teeth will fall out:* New York—TA, 1940s; American students in Tokyo—Simon, *WF* 12. VARIANT: Kentucky—This also will occur if one wears shoes with black soles, Thomas (2142). *Coins:* General. *Yawn:* General. *Saliva:* General.

p. 87 *Cross your fingers:* General.

p. 88 *Kiss your elbow:* New York—Reported by Jean Tracy, JA, 1945; American students in Tokyo—Simon, *WF* 12. VARIANT: Louisiana—If a girl kisses her toe she will become a boy, Roberts, *JAF* 40 (322).

Ailments and Cures

p. 89. *Onions:* Massachusetts—Bergen, MAFS 7, p. 114; Indiana

—Brewster, *SFQ* 3. VARIANT: Kentucky—Carry an onion in your pocket and you will stay healthy, Fowler, *SFQ* 14 (1425A). *Dime:* Alabama—Browne (2083). *Camphor:* General. *Potato:* General. *Garlic:* New York —Relihan, *NYFQ* 3. See discussion "Onions and garlic" in Notes. *Rainfall:* Southern United States—Puckett, p. 383.

p. 90 *Abracadabra:* General.

p. 91 *Stiff joints:* Kentucky—G. Wilson, *SFQ* 31. VARIANT: Kentucky, Ozark Mountains—Place worms in container in sun; heat until oil oozes, G. Wilson, *SFQ* 31; Randolph, *JAF* 46. *Stitch, crick:* Kentucky—Rub with a stone, G. Wilson, *SFQ* 30; Alabama—Spit on a stone, then put it back where you found it, Browne (1426).

p. 92 **Cold.** *Onions:* Kansas—Sackett, *WF* 20 (13). *Hog hoof:* Alabama—Browne (769). *Mule:* Sandburg, p. 162. VARIANT: Germany—Kissing a mule's nose is a cure for toothache, TA, 1940s. **Sore throat.** *Bacon:* New York—TA, 1940s, Tioga County. *Sock:* General. VARIANTS: General—Use thin slice of pork, peppered bacon, or skunk grease; Alabama—Use lemon slices, Browne (1697); Oregon—When thrust under the nose a "ripe" sock also stops snoring, Hines, *WF* 24 (68).

p. 93 *Chicken pox:* New York—TA, 1940s, Delaware County; Tennessee—Farr, *TFSB* 1; Kentucky—G. Wilson, *SFQ* 30.

p. 94 **Freckles.** *Watermelon juice:* New York—Reported by Catherine Relihan, JA, 1946. *Buttermilk:* General. *Blacksmith:* Ozark Mountains—Randolph, *JAF* 46. *Dew:* General. *Strawberries:* North Carolina—Hand (1503). *Cucumbers:* Maryland—UM, 1970. *Mud:* Maryland—Whitney (1522). *Manure:* Kentucky—G. Wilson, *SFQ* 31.

p. 95 **Warts.** *Bacon:* New York—"Farm Lore," *NYFQ* 3. *Dishrag:* General. *Bean:* General. *Pickle, onion:* Indiana—Halpert, *HF* 8. *Potato:* General. *Gizzard:* Kentucky—Pope, *KFR* 11. *Knot:* General. *Grapefruit:* American students in Tokyo—Simon, *WF* 12. *Rainwater:* Tennessee

149

—Hatcher, *SFQ* 19. *Spunk water:* Missouri—Twain, *The Adventures of Tom Sawyer*, reprint edition, p. 63. See discussion "Warts" in Notes.

p. 96 *Dead cat:* General.

p. 97 *Wart witch:* Texas—Wellborn, TXFS 30.

p. 98 **Hiccups.** *Hold your nose:* California—Funk, *WF* 9. *Far edge:* American students in Tokyo—Simon, *WF* 12. *Napkin:* California—Funk, *WF* 9. *Little fingers, hold your breath:* New York—JA, 1940s. VARIANT: Ozark Mountains—Stand on one leg, shout three times, "Hick-up, stick-up, lick-up, hick-up," Randolph, *JAF* 46. See discussion "Hiccups" in Notes.

p. 99 **Hair.** *Rum:* Maine—Beck, p. 45. *Wild grapes:* Ozark Mountains—Randolph, *JAF* 40. *Bread crusts, carrots:* Illinois—Hyatt (3638, 3639). *Beard:* New York— Barbara Carmer Schwartz, Princeton, N.J., learned of this danger during her childhood in Delmar, 1930s.

Animals, Birds, and Insects

p. 100, 101 **Black Cat.** *Pants:* New York—TA, 1940s. *Spit in hat:* General. *Spit in road:* Kentucky—Thomas (1032). *Cross arms:* New York—TA, 1940s. *Nine steps:* Idaho —Hand, *WF* 28 (24). *Go home:* Texas—Turner, TXFS 13.

p. 102 *Cats:* General.

p. 103 *Dog:* Maryland—UM, 1971; Kentucky—Thomas (3382).

p. 104 *Horsehair:* Pennsylvania—Belmont School, Philadelphia, 1971. *Horseshoe:* General. *Spit through prongs:* Kentucky—Pope, *KFR* 11; Tennessee—Frazier, *TFSB* 2.

p. 105 *Horseshoe:* General.

p. 106 *Rabbit's foot:* General. *To obtain:* Kentucky—Pope, *KFR* 11; North Carolina—Hand (5789–5804). *Left back pocket:* General. *Neck:* North Carolina—Hand (5790). *Older, drier:* Tennessee—Carter, *TFSB* 10.

p. 107 *Salt on the tail:* New York—JA, 1940s.

p. 108 *Owls:* General. *Clothes, shoes:* Texas—Turner, TXFS 13. *Pillowcase:* Tennessee—Hatcher, *SFQ* 19.

p. 109 *Blue jays:* Texas—Hendricks, *WF* 24; Colorado—Davidson, *WF* 13. *Don't you hear:* Ozark Mountains—Quoted in Randolph, p. 248.

p. 110 *Robin:* Tennessee—Farr, *JAF* 48; Ozark Mountains—Randolph, *JAF* 40. VARIANT: Colorado—Wish on the first robin you see, then stamp your wish (for technique see sources for p. 67), Davidson, *WF* 13.

p. 111 *Fly:* Maryland—UM, 1971; Illinois—Hyatt (1417). *Dragonfly:* New England—Johnson, p. 100. *Cricket:* General. *Relatives will eat:* California—Papashvily, *WF* 10.

p. 112 **Spider.** *News:* Kentucky—Pope, *KFR* 11; Illinois—Hyatt (1473). *Web:* Illinois—Hyatt (1487). *Initials:* Ozark Mountains—Randolph, *JAF* 46. Also see E. B. White, *Charlotte's Web* (New York: Harper & Row, 1952), in which a spider weaves messages and announcements in her web. *Quarrel:* New York—TA, 1940s. *Kill:* New York—TA, 1940s.

Plants

p. 113 *Catch a falling leaf:* Tennessee—Farr, *JAF* 48. VARIANT: England—The reward is one day's luck or a wish, Opie, p. 217.

p. 114 *Four-leaf clover:* General. *Shoe:* Wyoming—*WF* 9 (2). *Knock on wood:* General.

p. 115 **A daisy.** *"Yes," "No":* New Jersey—Churchill Junior High School, East Brunswick. VARIANT: General—"This year," "Next year," "Sometimes," "Never," Kell, *JAF* 69. **A dandelion.** *Time:* General. *Mother:* New England—Johnson, p. 53. *Punished:* Kentucky—Thomas (87).

p. 116 *Mistletoe:* General.

p. 117, 118 *Mandrake:* Jennings, p. 43.

p. 119 *Sunburned vegetables:* New York—TA, 1940s, Tioga County. *Potatoes and onions:* Maine—Unidentified farmer near Liberty, 1973; Illinois—Hyatt (1190).

The Weather

p. 120 *Groundhog:* General.

p. 121 *Moon:* General. *Cat sneezes:* General. *Yawns, licks its tail:* New York—TA, 1940s. *Eats grass:* Oregon—Hines, *WF* 24 (215). *Scratches:* New York—TA, 1940s. *Ant:* General. *Nose:* Maryland—UM, 1971. *Grapes:* Massachusetts—H. B. Wilson, *JAF* 16.

p. 122 *Robins:* New York—TA, 1940s. *Wasps, hornets:* Maine— Beck, p. 82; Tennessee—Page, *TSFB* 20. *Hogs:* Maine —Beck, p. 82. *Other animals, oaks:* General. *How cold:* New York—TA, 1940s. VARIANT: Ozark Mountains— Twice as many freezing days as sunny days the previous summer, Randolph, *JAF* 46. *How much snow:* New York—TA, 1940s; Ozark Mountains—Randolph, *JAF* 46. *Weather will be clear:* Kentucky—Thomas (2567).

Death

p. 123 *A warning:* General. *Dog howls:* Colorado—Earthman, *WF* 16. *Lies on back:* Alabama—Browne (3234); Illinois—Hyatt (14724). *Owl, whippoorwill:* General. *Picture drops:* Kansas—Koch, p. 82. *Rapping, knocking:* Oregon—Oregon WPA Folklore Files, *WF* 24 (1). *Ringing in ears:* Tennessee—Hatcher, *SFQ* 19; Carter, *TFSB* 10. The ringing also is called "death bells." *Falling star:* Washington—Hines, *WF* 24 (180). *Muddy water:* Tennessee—Hatcher, *SFQ* 19.

p. 124 *Bees:* Indiana—Dundes, *MF* 11; New Hampshire—Currier, *JAF* 2; North Carolina—Hand (7519). See discussion "Telling the bees" in Notes.

p. 125 *Funeral procession:* England—Opie, p. 215. *Count cars:* Kentucky—Thomas (759); Ozark Mountains—Randolph, *JAF* 40. *Each one you count:* Alabama— Browne (3167). *Graveyard:* New Jersey—Princeton

High School and Valley Road School, Princeton, 1973. *Point at a grave:* Pennsylvania—Belmont School, Philadelphia, 1972; Southern United States—Puckett, p. 312. *Stars:* Kentucky—Shearin, *JAF* 24. *Shiver:* American students in Tokyo—Simon, *WF* 12.

p. 126, 127 **Ghosts.** *Cold air, strange sounds, door:* General. *Lights:* North Carolina—Harden, p. 114. *Animal ghosts:* Ozark Mountains—Randolph, p. 223.

p. 128 *If you meet a ghost:* North Carolina—Hand (5725). VARIANT: New York—Say three times, "What dost thou want?" Jones, *JAF* 57.

The Moon and the Stars

p. 129, 130, 131 *Astrology:* General.

p. 132 *New moon:* New York—Reported by Mary Naylor, JA, 1945. VARIANT: Texas—If you see a new moon through a window, you will have bad luck through its entire phase, Turner, TXFS 13.

p. 133 *First star:* New York—Reported by Barbara Davenport, JA, 1945. VARIANTS: General—"Have the wish I wish tonight"; Ozark Mountains—"Star light, star bright/ First star I seen tonight/I wish I may, I wish I might/ Wish th' wish I wish tonight!" quoted in Randolph, *JAF* 46.

Bibliography

Books that may be of particular interest to young people are marked with an asterisk (*). Major collections of superstitions and other folk beliefs are marked with a dagger (†).

BOOKS

† Beck, Horace P. *The Folklore of Maine.* Philadelphia and New York: J. B. Lippincott Co., 1957.

Bergen, F. D. *Animal and Plant Lore.* Memoirs of the American Folklore Society 7. Boston: American Folklore Society, 1899.

Brown, Raymond L. *A Book of Superstitions.* Devon, England: David & Charles, 1970.

† Browne, Ray B. *Popular Beliefs and Practices from Alabama.* Folklore Studies 9. Berkeley and Los Angeles: University of California Press, 1958. *A collection of 4,340 beliefs.*

Chaundler, Christine. *Everyman's Book of Superstitions.* London: A. R. Mowbray & Co., 1970.

* Coffin, Tristram P. *The Old Ball Game.* New York: Herder and Herder, 1971. *A study of superstition in baseball.*

————, and Cohen, Hennig, eds. *Folklore in America.* New York: Doubleday & Co., 1966.

* Cohen, Daniel. *Superstition.* Mankato, Minn.: Creative Education Press, 1971.

The Columbia Encyclopedia. Edited by William Bridgewater and Seymour Kurtz. 3d ed. New York: Columbia University Press, 1963.

Creighton, Helen. *Folklore of Lumenburg County, Nova Scotia.* Bulletin 117, Anthropological Series 29. Ottawa: National Museum of Canada, 1950.

de Lys, Claudia. *A Treasury of American Superstitions.* New York: The Philosophical Library, 1948.

Dresslar, Fletcher B. *Superstitions and Education.* University of California Publications in Education 5. Berkeley, 1907.

* Emrich, Duncan. *The Hodgepodge Book.* New York: Four Winds Press, 1972. *An informal compendium of folk beliefs, proverbs, and other folklore, with a 50-page bibliography.*

* Emrich, Marion V., and Korson, George C. *The Child's Book of Folklore.* New York: The Dial Press, 1947.

† Frazer, Sir James George. *The Golden Bough: A Study in Magic and Religion.* New York: The Macmillan Company, 1969. *Abridged edition of a 13-volume study, one of the major scholarly works in modern history.*

† Gardner, Emelyn E. *Folklore from the Schoharie Hills, New York.* Ann Arbor, Mich.: University of Michigan Press, 1937.

* Grahame, Kenneth. *The Wind in the Willows.* New York: Charles Scribner's Sons, 1908.

† Hand, Wayland D., ed. *Popular Beliefs and Superstitions from North Carolina.* The Frank C. Brown Collection of North Carolina Folklore, vol. 6, 7. Durham, N.C.: Duke University Press, 1964. *An extensively annotated collection of 8,569 beliefs.*

* Harden, John. *Tar Heel Ghosts.* Chapel Hill, N.C.: University of North Carolina Press, 1954.

† Hyatt, Harry M. *Folk-lore from Adams County, Illinois.* Memoirs of the Alma Egan Hyatt Foundation. New York, 1935. 2d ed., Hannibal, Missouri, 1965. *With 16,537 entries, the largest single compilation of folk beliefs relating to the United States.*

Igglesden, Charles. *Those Superstitions.* London: Jarrolds Publishers, 1932. Reprint edition, Ann Arbor, Mich.: Gryphon Books, 1971.

Jahoda, Gustav. *The Psychology of Superstition.* London: The Penguin Press, 1971.

* Jennings, Gary. *Black Magic, White Magic.* New York: The Dial Press, 1964.

† Johnson, Clifton. *What They Say in New England and Other American Folklore.* Boston: Lee and Shepherd, 1896. Reprint

edition, ed. Carl A. Withers. New York: Columbia University Press, 1963. *One of the first comprehensive folklore collections in the United States.*

Kittredge, George L. *Witchcraft in Old and New England.* Cambridge, Mass.: Harvard University Press, 1929.

Knortz, Karl. *Amerikanischer Aberglaube der Gegenwart: Ein Beitrag zur Volkskunde.* Leipzig: T. Gerstenberg, 1913.

Koch, William E., and Sackett, Sidney J. *Kansas Folklore.* Lincoln, Neb.: University of Nebraska Press, 1961.

* Leach, Maria. *The Luck Book.* Cleveland and New York: World Publishing Co., 1964.

Maple, Eric. *Superstition and the Superstitious.* London: W. H. Allen, 1971.

†* Opie, Iona and Peter. *The Lore and Language of Schoolchildren.* London and New York: Oxford University Press, 1959. *A classic account of children's folklore in England and Scotland.*

† Puckett, Newbell N. *Folk Beliefs of the Southern Negro.* Chapel Hill: University of North Carolina Press, 1926.

† Randolph, Vance. *Ozark Superstitions.* New York: Columbia University Press, 1947. *Folk beliefs in the Ozark Mountains in the 1920s and 1930s.*

Sandburg, Carl. *Always the Young Strangers.* New York: Harcourt, Brace & Co., 1953.

Schmidt, Philippe. *Superstition and Magic.* Cork, Ireland: The Mercier Press, 1963.

Standard Dictionary of Folklore, Mythology, and Legend. Edited by Maria Leach. 2 vols. New York: Funk & Wagnalls, 1949.

† Thomas, Daniel L. and Lucy B. *Kentucky Superstitions.* Princeton, N.J.: Princeton University Press, 1920. *A collection of 3,954 beliefs.*

* Twain, Mark [pseud. of Clemens, Samuel L.]. *The Adventures of Huckleberry Finn.* New York: Charles L. Webster & Co., 1883. Reprint edition, New York: The Heritage Press, 1952.

* ———. *The Adventures of Tom Sawyer.* Hartford, Conn.: American Publishing Co., 1876. Reprint edition, New York: The Heritage Press, 1952.

Waterman, Philip F. *The Story of Superstition*. New York: Alfred A. Knopf, 1929.

Whitney, Annie W., and Bullock, Caroline C. *Folklore from Maryland*. Memoirs of the American Folklore Society 25. New York: American Folklore Society, 1925.

ARTICLES

Abrahams, Roger D. "A Rhetoric of Traditional Conversational Genres." *SFQ* 32 (1968): 44–59.

Allen, Lee. "The Superstitions of Baseball Players." *NYFQ* 20 (1964): 98–109.

Allen, Prudence. "Love and Marriage in York State Lore." *NYFQ* 5 (1949): 257–267.

Barker, Addison. "Anatomical Superstitions in Blum's Almanac." *NCF* 8 (1960): 47–48.

Beckwith, Martha W. "Signs and Superstitions Collected from American College Girls." *JAF* 36 (1923): 1–15.

Boughton, Audrey. "Weather Lore: Spring Quarter." *NYFQ* 1 (1945): 123–125.

———. "Weather Lore: Summer Quarter." *NYFQ* 1 (1945): 189–90.

Brewster, Paul G. "Folk Cures and Preventives from Southern Indiana." *SFQ* 3 (1939): 33–43.

Bryan, Naomi R. "Children's Customs in San Mateo." *WF* 8 (1949): 261.

Bryant, Margaret M. "Folklore from Edgefield County, South Carolina: Beliefs, Superstitions, Dreams." *SFQ* 13 (1949): 136–148.

Busse, Norma. "Superstitions of the Theater." *WF* 8 (1949): 66–67.

Carter, Roland C. "Mountain Superstitions." *TFSB* 10, no. 1 (1944): 1–6.

Combs, Josiah H. "Sympathetic Magic in the Kentucky Mountains." *JAF* 27 (1914): 328–330.

Currier, John M. "Contributions to the Folk-Lore of New England." *JAF* 2 (1889): 291–294.

Davidson, Levette J. "Folk Beliefs in Southern Indiana." *WF* 16 (1957): 204.

————. "Superstitions Collected in Denver, Colorado." *WF* 13 (1954): 184–189.

† Dundes, Alan. "Brown County Superstitions." *MF* 11 (1961): 25–55. *A collection of 219 annotated beliefs.*

Earthman, George. "Superstitions from Denver." *WF* 16 (1957): 132–133.

Elliot, Frances. "Stagestruck Luck." *KFR* 10 (1964): 18–21.

"Farm Lore." *NYFQ* 3 (1947): 256–258. *Wart cures.*

† Farr, T. J. "Middle Tennessee Folk Beliefs Concerning Love and Marriage." *SFQ* 2 (1938): 165–174. *A collection of 190 items.*

† ————. "Riddles and Superstitions of Middle Tennessee." *JAF* 48 (1935): 318–336.

————. "Survivals of Superstitions in Tennessee." *TFSB* 21, no. 1 (1955): 1–3.

————. "Tennessee Folk Beliefs Concerning Children." *JAF* 52 (1939): 112–116.

————. "Tennessee Superstitions and Beliefs." *TFSB* 1, no. 2 (1935): 14–27.

Foster, James R. "Brooklyn Folklore." *NYFQ* 13 (1957): 83–91.

Foster, Jerry. "Varieties of Sea Lore." *WF* 28 (1969): 260–266.

Fowler, David C. and Mary G. "More Kentucky Superstitions." *SFQ* 14 (1950): 170–176. *A supplement to Thomas, Kentucky Superstitions.*

Frazier, Neal. "A Collection of Middle Tennessee Superstitions." *TFSB* 2, no. 4 (1936): 33–48.

Funk, William D. "Hiccup Cures." *WF* 9 (1950): 66–67.

Granger, Byrd H. "Of the Teeth." *JAF* 74 (1961): 47–56.

Gross, Dan. "Folklore of the Theater." *WF* 20 (1961): 257–263.

Halpert, Violetta. "Indiana Wart Cures." *HF* 8 (1949): 37–43.

Hand, Wayland D. " 'The Fear of Gods': Superstition and Popular Belief." Chapter 19, *Our Living Traditions*, ed. Tristram P. Coffin. New York: Basic Books, 1968.

————. "Folk Beliefs from Boise, Idaho." *WF* 28 (1969): 41–42.

Hatcher, Mildred. "Superstitions in Middle Tennessee." *SFQ* 19 (1955): 150–155.

Hendricks, George D. "More Texas Superstitions." *WF* 24 (1965): 111–113.

† Hines, Donald M. "Superstitions from Oregon." *WF* 24 (1965): 7–20. *A collection of 216 annotated beliefs.*
Jagendorf, Moritz A. "Apples in Life and Lore." *NYFQ* 18 (1962): 273–283.
Jones, Louis C. "The Evil Eye Among European-Americans." *WF* 10 (1951): 11–25.
————. "The Ghosts of New York: An Analytical Study." *JAF* 57 (1944): 237–254.
Kell, Katherine T. "The Folklore of the Daisy." *JAF* 69 (1956): 369–376.
Lowrimore, Burton. "California Superstitions." *CFQ* 4 (1945): 178.
McCadden, Helen M. "Folklore in the Schools." *NYFQ* 3 (1947): 330–340. *Beliefs in a New York City high school.*
Miller, William M. "How to Become a Witch." *JAF* 57 (1944): 280.
Mills, Randolph V. "Superstitions." *WF* 11 (1952): 43–45. *Mid-nineteenth-century California superstitions.*
Naff, Alixa. "Belief in the Evil Eye among the Christian Syrian-Lebanese in America." *JAF* 78 (1965): 46–51.
Odell, Ruth. "Mid-Western Saliva Lore." *SFQ* 14 (1950): 220–223.
Oregon WPA Folklore Files. "Oregon Death and Funerary Beliefs." *WF* 24 (1965): 6.
Owens, Ethel. "Witchcraft in the Cumberlands." *KFR* 11 (1965): 76–77.
Page, Marion T. "Superstitions at Home." *TFSB* 20, no. 3 (1954): 53–56.
Papashvily, Helen. "The World in a California Street: Stockton, 1911–1920." *WF* 10 (1951): 117–125.
Penrod, James H. "Folk Beliefs About Work, Trades, and Professions from New Mexico." *WF* 27 (1968): 180–183.
† Pope, Genevieve. "Superstitions and Beliefs in Fleming County." *KFR* 11 (1965): 41–49. *A collection of 204 Kentucky beliefs.*
† Randolph, Vance. "Folk-Beliefs in the Ozark Mountains." *JAF* 40 (1927): 78–93.
† ————. "Ozark Superstitions." *JAF* 46 (1933): 1–21.
Relihan, Catherine M. "Farm Lore: Folk Remedies." *NYFQ* 3 (1947): Part I, 81–84; Part II, 166–169.

† Roberts, Hilda. "Louisiana Superstitions." *JAF* 40 (1927): 114–208. *A collection of 1,585 beliefs.*

Rumley, Barbara C. "Superstitions in San Francisco." *WF* 9 (1950): 159–160.

Sackett, S. J. "Folk Medicine from West Kansas." *WF* 20 (1961): 256.

————. "More Folk Medicine from Kansas." *WF* 23 (1964): 76.

————. "Signs of Bad Luck from Western Kansas." *WF* 23 (1964): 240.

Shearin, H. G. "Some Superstitions in the Cumberland Mountains." *JAF* 24 (1911): 319–322.

Simon, Gladys H. "Beliefs and Customs Reported by Students at Tokyo American School." *WF* 12 (1953): 85–93.

Tullis, C. O. "Folk Beliefs from Mt. Ayr High School." *HF* 5 (1946): 35–36.

† Turner, Tressa. "The Human Comedy in Folk Superstitions." In *Straight Texas.* TXFS 13. Austin: Texas Folk-Lore Society, 1937.

Walton, Miranda S. "Wyoming Pioneer Superstitions." *WF* 9 (1950): 161–162.

Wellborn, Grace P. "The Magic Art of Removing Warts." In *Singers and Storytellers.* TXFS 30. Dallas: Southern Methodist University Press, 1961. *Account of a wart witch.*

Wilson, Eddie W. "The Onion in Folk Belief." *WF* 12 (1953): 94–104.

Wilson, Gordon. "Swallow It or Rub It On: More Mammoth Cave Remedies." *SFQ* 31 (1967): 296–303.

————. "Talismans and Magic in Folk Remedies in the Mammoth Cave Region." *SFQ* 30 (1966): 192–201.

Wilson, Howard B. "Notes of Syrian Folk-Lore Collected in Boston." *JAF* 16 (1903): 133–147.

Wine, Martin L. "Superstitions Collected in Chicago." *MF* 7 (1947): 149–159.

Woodall, N. F. "Old Signs in Alabama." *JAF* 43 (1930): 325–326.

An Acknowledgment

Many people helped in creating this book. They include the following:

The late Velma V. Varner, who some years ago as my editor helped shape my thinking about such a work.

Professor Bruce R. Buckley of the Cooperstown Graduate Programs and Mrs. Marion Brophey of the New York State Historical Association, who made it possible for me to study the Louis C. Jones and Harold W. Thompson Archives.

Professor Esther K. Birdsall, Mrs. Geraldine Johnson, and Nathan Olivera of the University of Maryland, who did the same at the Maryland Folklore Archives.

Professor Kenneth S. Goldstein of the Department of Folklore and Folklife at the University of Pennsylvania, who made available his personal library of folklore.

Folklorists and folklore students whose work was a significant source of information and insight.

Persons who contributed their superstitions: individuals in Maine communities, students at Rutgers University, and young people in Philadelphia and in Princeton and East Brunswick, N.J.

Librarians at Princeton University, Rutgers University, the University of Maine, and the Princeton, N.J., Public Library.

My daughter Elizabeth, who read my manuscript from the viewpoint of a young person and made valuable suggestions regarding its content and clarity.

Folklore societies and publishing firms which provided permission to use copyrighted materials.

I am grateful to each.

A.S.

About Alvin Schwartz

Alvin Schwartz is the author of many books for young
people that deal with subjects as varied as folklore,
crafts, museums, labor unions, and urban problems. He
teaches a writing workshop at Rutgers University. He
also writes in a small studio in Princeton, New Jersey,
next to the house where he lives with his wife, four children, and two black cats.

About Glen Rounds

Glen Rounds spent his childhood on ranches in South
Dakota and Montana. He attended art school in Kansas
City, Missouri, and in New York City, and now lives in
Southern Pines, North Carolina. He has illustrated many
books for young people. This is his fourth collaboration
with Alvin Schwartz.

Also by Alvin Schwartz and Glen Rounds

A Twister of Twists, A Tangler of Tongues
Tomfoolery: Trickery and Foolery with Words
Witcracks: Jokes and Jests from American Folklore